BlueWild Education

Alphabet of the Sea

Written and Illustrated by
Ashleigh Rutter

Written and illustrated by Ashleigh Rutter
Published by BlueWild Press

ISBN: 978-1-7646732-0-4
First published in 2026
Printed on demand

A a   Angelfish

ayn-gul fish

Angelfish come in many bright colours!

B b   Blue whale

bloo wayl

Blue whales are the biggest animals on Earth!

C c   Clownfish

klown-fish

Clownfish stay safe by hiding in stinging anemones!

D d

Dolphin

dol-fin

Dolphins speak through clicks and whistles!

E e

Eel

eel

Eels open their mouths to pump water over their gills!

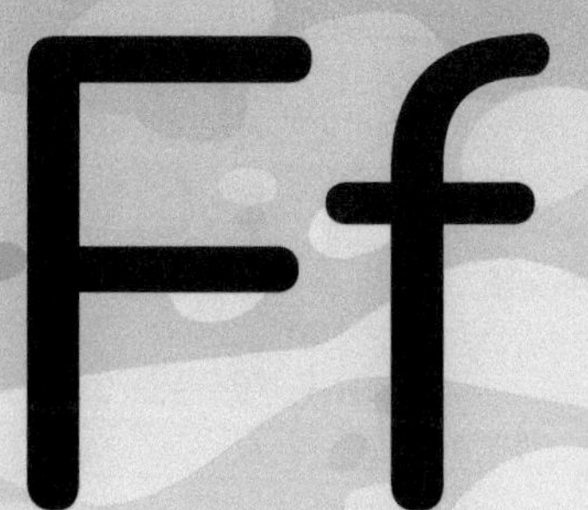

Ff

Flounder

floun-duh

Flounders have both eyes on one side of their head!

G g Guitarfish

gih-tar-fish

Guitarfish look like a mix between a shark and a ray!

Hh Hammer-head shark

ham-uh-hed shark

Hammerheads can see in lots of directions at once!

Ii

Indian mackeral

in-dee-un mak-er-ul

Indian mackeral swim in big schools with all their friends!

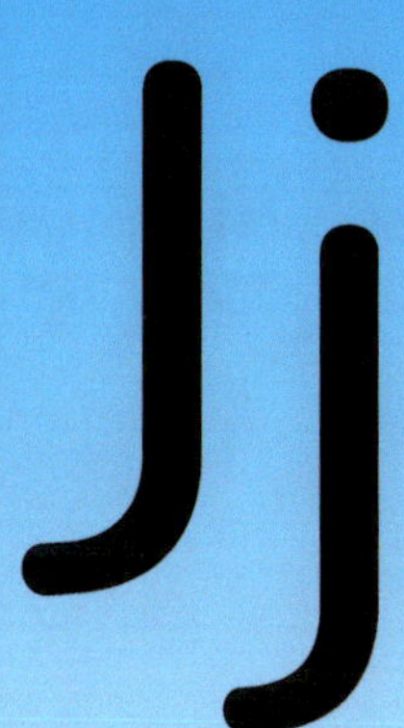

Jj

Jellyfish
jell-ee-fish

Jellyfish float in the water, drifting with the current!

K k Killer whale

kil-uh wayl

Killer whales have families that stay together for life!

L l

Lionfish

lie-un-fish

Lionfish spread their spines as a warning to stay away!

Mm Manta ray

man-tuh ray

Manta rays visit cleaning stations to be cleaned by tiny fish

Nn Nudibranch

noo-dee-brank

Nudibranchs are tiny sea slugs covered in bright colours!

Oo 

Octopus

ok-tuh-puss

Octopuses can change colour when they're scared!

P p   Pufferfish

puff-uh-fish

Pufferfish can 'puff' up like a balloon when surprised!

Q q Queensland grouper
qweens-lund groop-uh
Queensland groupers can grow bigger than a person!

Rr   Ray
ray

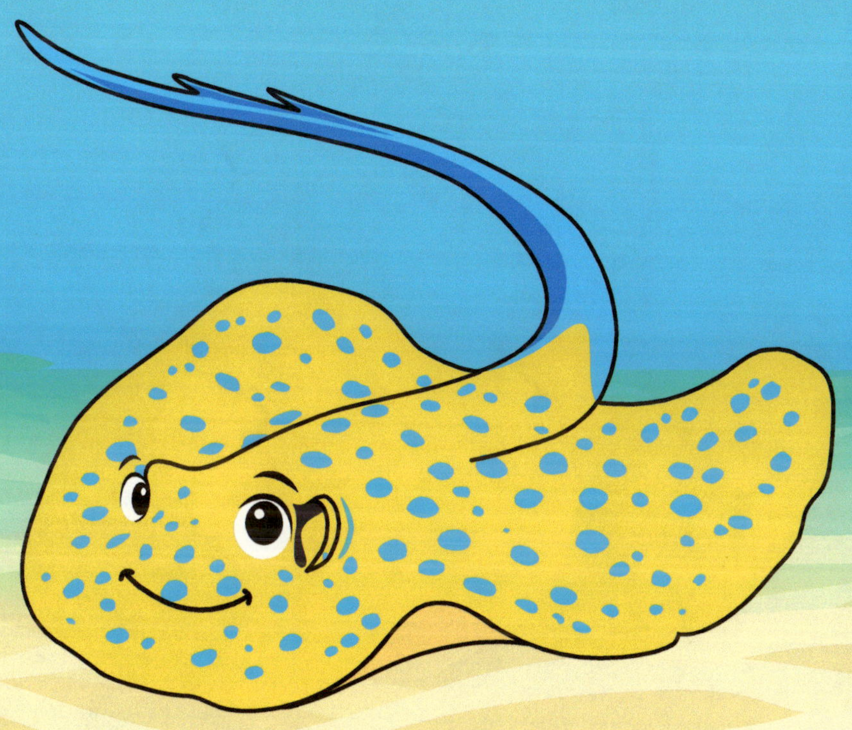

ays like to hide under the sand with their eyes poking out!

Ss Seahorse

see-haws

Seahorses like to cling to seaweed so they dont drift away

T t   Turtle

tur-tel

Turtles like to rest on rocks and corals when they're tired!

U u Unicornfish

yoo-nih-korn fish

Unicorn fish get their name from the bump on their heads

Vv

Vampire squid

vam-pie-uh skwid

Vampire squids eat 'marine snow' and can glow in the dark!

W w Whale shark

way-l shark

Whale sharks are gentle giants that eat tiny plankton!

Xx Xiphias (Swordfish)

ziff-ee-us (sord-fish)

Swordfish can heat their eyes to see better in cold water!

Yy

Yellowfin tuna

yel-oh-fin too-nuh

Yellowfin tuna never stop swimming!

Zz Zebra shark

zeb-ruh shark

Zebra sharks have stripes as babies and spots as adults!

Keep exploring with Bluewild Education

More ocean-themed early-learning books are on the way!

Follow along on Instagram:

@bluewildpress